15-Minute Foodie

Vegetarian Recipes in 15 Minutes or Less

by Tamara JM Peterson

CAPSTONE PRESS
a capstone imprint

Dabble Lab is published by Capstone Press, an imprint of Capstone.
1710 Roe Crest Drive, North Mankato, Minnesota 56003
capstonepub.com

Copyright © 2024 by Capstone. All rights reserved. No part of this publication may be reproduced in whole or in part, or stored in a retrieval system, or transmitted in any form or by any means, electronic, mechanical, photocopying, recording, or otherwise, without written permission of the publisher.

Library of Congress Cataloging-in-Publication Data
Names: Peterson, Tamara JM, author.
Title: Vegetarian recipes in 15 minutes or less / by Tamara JM Peterson.
Description: North Mankato, Minnesota : Capstone Press, a Capstone imprint, [2024] | Series: 15-minute foodie | Includes bibliographical references. | Audience: Ages 8-11 | Audience: Grades 4-6 | Summary: "Looking to serve up quick and delicious vegetarian recipes? Become a 15-minute foodie! Make a crispy egg roll loaded with avocado. Scoop up zesty fruit salsa onto cinnamon sugar tortilla chips. Swap out meat for lentils to build a vegetarian sloppy joe. These quick, fun, yummy recipes will be ready to enjoy in 15 minutes or less"— Provided by publisher.
Identifiers: LCCN 2023023929 (print) | LCCN 2023023930 (ebook) | ISBN 9781669061717 (hardcover) | ISBN 9781669061670 (pdf) | ISBN 9781669061694 (kindle edition) | ISBN 9781669061687 (epub)
Subjects: LCSH: Cooking (Vegetables)—Juvenile literature. | Quick and easy cooking—Juvenile literature. | LCGFT: Cookbooks
Classification: LCC TX801 .P496 2024 (print) | LCC TX801 (ebook) | DDC 641.5/636—dc23/eng/20230524
LC record available at https://lccn.loc.gov/2023023929
LC ebook record available at https://lccn.loc.gov/2023023930

Image Credits
Adobe Stock: Dionisvera, 7 (apple and cinnamon sticks), sveta, Front Cover (avocado); iStockphoto: monkeybusinessimages, 4, PeopleImages, 5; Mighty Media, Inc.: project photos

Design Elements
iStockphoto: Sirintra_Pumsopa, yugoro; Mighty Media, Inc.

Editorial Credits
Editor: Jessica Rusick
Designers: Sarah DeYoung and Denise Hamernik
Cook: Chelsey Luciow

All internet sites appearing in back matter were available and accurate when this book was sent to press.

The publisher and the author shall not be liable for any damages allegedly arising from the information in this book, and they specifically disclaim any liability from the use or application of any of the contents of this book.

Printed and bound in China. 5593

Table of Contents

Vegetarian Recipes in Fifteen! 4
Raw Apple Pie 6
Fruit Salsa with Cinnamon Chips . . . 8
PB&J Bistro Box 10
Lentil Tacos 12
Veggie Ramen 14
Loaded Bean Burritos 16
Caprese Panini 18
Veggie Wraps 20
Lentil Sloppy Joes 22
Veggie Fried Rice 24
Chocolate Date Bites 26
Roasted Chickpeas 28
Avocado Egg Rolls 30
    Read More 32
    Internet Sites 32
    About the Author 32

Vegetarian Recipes in Fifteen!

Are you looking for fun vegetarian recipes to add some excitement to your snacks and meals? Whether you're in the mood for tacos, fried rice, a veggie wrap, or chocolate-covered dates, this book is full of ideas to satisfy your cravings. And the best part is, these recipes come together in 15 minutes or less! So grab your kitchen supplies and read through the tips on the next page. Soon enough, you'll be a 15-minute foodie!

Basic Supplies

- baking sheet
- frying pan
- knife and cutting board
- meal prep container
- measuring cups and spoons
- mixing bowls
- paper towels
- pizza cutter
- spatula
- spoon
- strainer
- toothpicks

Kitchen Tips

Ask an adult for permission before you make a recipe.

Read through the recipe and set out all ingredients and supplies before you start cooking.

Using metric tools? Use the conversion chart below to make your recipe measure up.

Wash your hands before and after you handle food. Wash and dry fresh produce before use.

Ask an adult for help when using a knife, blender, or stovetop. Wear oven mitts when removing items from the oven or microwave.

When you are done making food, clean your work surface. Wash dirty dishes and put all supplies and ingredients back where you found them.

Standard	Metric
¼ teaspoon	1.25 grams or milliliters
½ teaspoon	2.5 g or mL
1 teaspoon	5 g or mL
1 tablespoon	15 g or mL
¼ cup	57 g (dry) or 60 mL (liquid)
⅓ cup	75 g (dry) or 80 mL (liquid)
½ cup	114 g (dry) or 125 mL (liquid)
⅔ cup	150 g (dry) or 160 mL (liquid)
¾ cup	170 g (dry) or 175 mL (liquid)
1 cup	227 g (dry) or 240 mL (liquid)
1 quart	950 mL

Raw Apple Pie

This fresh, crunchy treat is a fun and healthy twist on apple pie.

Ingredients

1 apple, peeled and finely chopped
2 tablespoons lemon juice
2 large dates
2 to 3 tablespoons walnuts, chopped
1½ tablespoons cinnamon
½ tablespoon honey

Supplies

peeler
knife and cutting board
measuring spoons
bowl
spoon

1. Put all the ingredients into the bowl.

2. Mix the ingredients together and put the bowl in the refrigerator.

3. Let the mixture chill for at least ten minutes. Then eat your sweet and simple treat!

Food Tip

If you prefer a sweeter treat, add an extra tablespoon of dates to the apple pie!

7

Fruit Salsa with Cinnamon Chips

This simple snack is the perfect combination of sweet, tangy, crunchy, and sweet.

Ingredients

¼ cup butter
1 tablespoon cinnamon
½ cup sugar
3 large flour tortillas
3 cups finely chopped fruit (bananas, strawberries, apples, and blueberries)
2 tablespoons lemon juice

Supplies

knife and cutting board
microwave-safe bowl
spoon
measuring cups and spoons
table knife
pizza cutter
parchment paper
baking sheet
large mixing bowl
serving platter

1. Preheat the oven to 350 degrees Fahrenheit (177 degrees Celsius).

2. Place the butter in the microwave-safe bowl. Melt the butter in the microwave. Stir the cinnamon and sugar into the butter.

3. Spread the butter mixture onto the tortillas with the table knife.

4. Cut the tortillas into triangular chips using the pizza cutter.

5. Place the tortilla chips on the parchment-lined baking sheet. Bake them for 10 minutes.

6. While the chips are baking, combine the fruit and lemon juice in the large bowl.

7. Remove the chips from the oven. Serve them on the platter with your fruit salsa!

9

PB&J Bistro Box

Grab a meal prep container and pack a simple vegetarian lunch to take on the go.

Ingredients

3 slices whole wheat bread
1 tablespoon peanut butter
1 tablespoon jam
2 celery stalks, chopped
½ cup baby carrots
½ cup strawberries, halved
½ cup blueberries

Supplies

knife and cutting board
measuring cups and spoons
table knife
meal prep container

1. Spread jam on one slice of bread with the table knife.

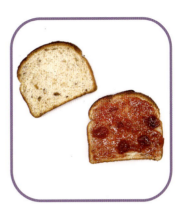

2. Place the second slice of bread on top.

3. Spread peanut butter on the third slice of bread.

4. Place the third slice of bread, peanut butter side down, on top of the first two slices to make the PB&J sandwich.

5. Cut the PB&J sandwich into fourths.

6. Place the sandwich, celery, carrots, strawberries, and blueberries into the meal prep container. Your lunch is ready to take on the road!

Lentil Tacos

Who needs meat? These delicious vegetarian tacos will be the hit of any Taco Tuesday.

Ingredients

1 tablespoon olive oil
¼ cup yellow onion, diced
15-ounce can brown lentils, drained and rinsed
½ cup frozen cauliflower rice
½ packet taco seasoning
¼ cup vegetable broth
6-ounce can tomato paste
½ tablespoon Worcestershire sauce
3 crunchy taco shells
½ cup shredded cheese
½ cup shredded lettuce
1 tomato, diced

Supplies

knife and cutting board
strainer
measuring cups and spoons
frying pan
spatula

1. Heat the oil in the frying pan over medium heat.

2. Cook the onion in the frying pan until it is golden brown, stirring occasionally.

3. Stir in the lentils, rice, and taco seasoning. Cook the mixture for two minutes.

4. Add the vegetable broth, tomato paste, and Worcestershire sauce. Turn the heat down to low and let the mixture simmer for five minutes, stirring occasionally.

5. Add the filling to the taco shells. Top the tacos with cheese, lettuce, and tomato. Then dig in!

Veggie Ramen

Instant ramen noodles are quick and tasty. But with a few extra ingredients, you can upgrade simple ramen into a next-level meal.

Ingredients

- 2 instant ramen noodle packages (soy sauce or other vegetarian flavor)
- 3 cups vegetable broth
- 1 tablespoon sesame oil
- ½ cup carrots, julienned
- ¼ cup corn
- ¼ cup peas
- 1 cup bean sprouts (optional)
- 2 stalks green onion, chopped (optional)

Supplies

- knife and cutting board
- pot
- water
- spoon
- strainer
- measuring cups and spoons
- serving bowl

Food Fact!
To julienne ingredients means to cut them into thin strips.

1. Fill the pot halfway with water. Add the ramen noodles. Set the seasoning packets aside.

2. Heat the pot of noodles on high, stirring occasionally.

3. Once the water boils, remove the pot from the stove and strain the noodles. Pour the noodles back into the empty pot.

4. Heat the pot on low. Add the vegetable broth, sesame oil, carrots, corn, peas, and seasoning packets. Stir to combine.

5. Let the ramen simmer for three to five minutes.

6. If you'd like, serve your ramen in bowls garnished with bean sprouts and green onion!

Loaded Bean Burritos

These simple burritos come together quickly and pack a flavorful punch.

Ingredients

2 large flour tortillas
16-ounce can vegetarian refried beans
15-ounce can beans, drained and rinsed (pinto, white, or black)
2 tablespoons cilantro, chopped, plus optional extra for serving
¼ cup red onion, diced
1 tablespoon lime juice
1 tablespoon mild green chilis, diced (optional)
½ cup shredded cheese
avocado slices (optional)
tomato slices (optional)

Supplies

knife and cutting board
strainer
measuring cups and spoons
bowl
spoon
paper towels
water
microwave-safe plate

1. Spread the refried beans onto the tortillas. Leave about 1 inch (2.5 centimeters) of space along the edges.

2. Mix the regular beans, cilantro, red onion, and lime juice in the bowl. Stir in green chilis if you'd like.

3. Scoop ½ cup of the mixture onto each tortilla.

4. Top each tortilla with the shredded cheese.

5. Fold the sides of each tortilla in slightly. Roll the tortillas from bottom to top.

6. Wrap each burrito in a damp paper towel. Microwave the burritos on the microwave-safe plate one at a time for one to two minutes.

7. If you'd like, serve your burritos with avocado slices, tomato slices, and extra cilantro on the side!

Caprese Panini

A panini is a sandwich made with Italian bread.
It is often toasted and served warm.
This crispy panini is delicious enough to rival any deli's!

Ingredients

1 ciabatta roll
4 fresh mozzarella slices
pepper to taste
2 to 3 tomato slices
salt to taste
3 to 4 fresh basil leaves, stems removed
1 tablespoon balsamic glaze
½ tablespoon butter or olive oil

Supplies

knife and cutting board
measuring spoons
grill pan
large pot or pan lid
spatula

1. Slice the ciabatta roll in half lengthwise.

2. Lay the mozzarella slices on the bottom half of the roll. Sprinkle them with pepper.

3. Lay the tomato slices on top of the cheese. Sprinkle them with salt.

4. Place the basil leaves on the top of the tomato.

5. Drizzle the balsamic glaze on the inside of the top roll. Set it on the bottom roll.

6. Heat the butter or oil in the pan over medium-high heat.

7. Place the panini in the pan. Place the lid on top to squish it down.

8. Cook the panini for three minutes or until the bread starts to brown.

9. Flip the panini and cook for an additional two minutes. Enjoy the panini while it's warm!

Veggie Wraps

Mix and match your favorite vegetables to make fresh and simple tortilla wraps.

Ingredients

1 avocado
2 large flour tortillas
⅓ cup hummus
1 cup baby spinach leaves
½ cup carrots, julienned
½ cucumber, sliced
salt and pepper to taste
1 tablespoon olive oil

Supplies

knife and cutting board
measuring cups and spoons
4 toothpicks

Food Tip

Add or swap out ingredients to customize your wrap! Try lettuce, red onion, and tomato for fillings. Use mayonnaise as a base and balsamic glaze for a burst of tangy flavor!

1. Cut the avocado in half and remove the pit. Cut the flesh into thin slices while it's still in the peel. Scoop out the slices and set them aside.

2. Spread hummus onto each tortilla.

3. Cover the hummus with the avocado, spinach leaves, carrots, and cucumber.

4. Sprinkle the filling with salt and pepper. Then drizzle olive oil on top.

5. Roll up the wraps. Use the toothpicks to hold each wrap together. Then slice the wraps in half diagonally. Remove the toothpicks before eating!

Lentil Sloppy Joes

Swap ground beef for lentils in a vegetarian twist on a fun, classic meal.

Ingredients

15-ounce can brown lentils, drained and rinsed
6-ounce can tomato paste
water
1 packet sloppy joe seasoning
2 hamburger buns, sliced
2 tablespoons pickles, sliced

Supplies

knife and cutting board
frying pan
spoon
measuring spoons

1. Warm the frying pan over medium heat.

2. Add the lentils and tomato paste to the pan. Fill the tomato paste can halfway with water. Pour the water into the pan and stir the mixture.

3. Stir in the sloppy joe seasoning. Cook the mixture for five minutes.

4. Scoop the sloppy joe mix onto the bottom buns. Top with pickles.

5. Place the top buns onto the sloppy joes and dig in!

Food Fact!

Sloppy joes were invented in the early 1900s. Some claim the ground beef and tomato sauce sandwiches were invented in Sioux City, Iowa.

23

Veggie Fried Rice

This loaded fried rice works as a side dish or as its own meal!

Ingredients

2 tablespoons olive or vegetable oil
1 cup carrots, julienned
1 cup yellow onion, chopped
4 cloves garlic, minced
1 tablespoon fresh ginger, minced
1½ cups broccoli, chopped
¾ cup peas
¾ cup corn
2 eggs
1½ cups cooked brown rice
1½ tablespoons soy sauce
½ tablespoon sesame oil

Supplies

knife and cutting board
frying pan
measuring cups and spoons
spatula
small bowl
fork

Food Tip

Use a wok to cook your fried rice if possible! These deep, rounded pans trap heat and speed the cooking process.

1. Heat the oil in the pan over medium-high heat.

2. Add the carrots, onion, garlic, ginger, broccoli, peas, and corn to the pan. Cook the vegetables until they are soft, stirring occasionally.

3. Push the vegetables to one half of the pan.

4. Crack the eggs into the small bowl. Whisk them together with the fork to break the yolks.

5. Pour the eggs into the empty half of the pan.

6. Let the eggs cook for two minutes. Mix and break up the eggs to scramble them.

7. When the eggs are firm, stir them into the vegetables. Then stir the rice, soy sauce, and sesame oil into the pan. Cook the rice for two minutes. Then serve!

Chocolate Date Bites

Dates are a sweet, healthy fruit. Add chocolate, peanut butter, and banana to make them even more delicious!

Ingredients

11 dates, pitted
2 tablespoons chunky peanut butter
1 banana, sliced into 11 pieces
½ cup dark chocolate chips
1 teaspoon vegetable oil

Supplies

knife and cutting board
measuring cups and spoons
11 toothpicks
microwave-safe bowl
spoon
parchment paper
baking sheet

1. Fill each date with ½ teaspoon peanut butter and one banana slice.

2. Place the chocolate chips and oil in the microwave-safe bowl. Microwave the mixture in 15-second bursts, stirring after each one, until the chocolate is melted and smooth.

3. Pierce each date with a toothpick to hold it closed. Dip each date into the melted chocolate.

4. Place the dipped dates onto the parchment-lined baking sheet. Place the sheet in the freezer for 10 minutes or until the chocolate sets. Then enjoy your sweet treats!

Roasted Chickpeas

Have a little more than 15 minutes? Make this sweet snack that's healthy and fun to eat.

Ingredients

15-ounce can chickpeas, drained
1 teaspoon vegetable or olive oil
1 teaspoon cinnamon
½ teaspoon vanilla
¼ teaspoon salt
1 tablespoon maple syrup or honey
fresh fruit (optional)

Supplies

strainer
measuring spoons
bowl
parchment paper
baking sheet

1. Preheat the oven to 325 degrees Fahrenheit (163°C).

2. Stir the chickpeas, oil, cinnamon, vanilla, salt, and maple syrup or honey together in the bowl.

3. Spread the mixture on the parchment-lined baking sheet and bake for 12 to 15 minutes.

4. Serve the chickpeas warm or at room temperature! If you'd like, serve fresh fruit on the side. Store extra chickpeas in an airtight container for up to three days.

Food Fact!

Chickpeas are also called garbanzo beans. They are filled with protein and other important nutrients!

Avocado Egg Rolls

Do you have a little extra time to cook? Try these creamy, crispy avocado egg rolls.

Ingredients

3 avocados
juice of 1 lime
salt and pepper to taste
1 tomato, chopped
¼ cup red onion, chopped
2 tablespoons cilantro, chopped, plus optional extra for serving
8 egg roll wrappers
¼ cup olive oil
fresh vegetables (optional)

Supplies

knife and cutting board
spoon
bowl
fork
measuring cups and spoons
water
parchment paper
baking sheet
basting brush

1. Preheat the oven to 425 degrees Fahrenheit (218°C).

2. Cut the avocados in half and remove the pits. Scoop the flesh into the bowl. Add the lime juice and salt and pepper.

3. Mash the avocado with the fork.

4. Add the tomato, red onion, and cilantro to the bowl. Stir the ingredients together.

5. Scoop about one-eighth of the filling onto the bottom edge of a wrapper.

6. Roll the bottom of the wrapper over the filling. Then fold in the sides and continue to roll up to the top.

7. Rub a drop of water along the top edge of the wrapper and press to seal.

8. Repeat steps 5 through 7 with the other wrappers.

9. Place the egg rolls on the parchment-lined baking sheet. Brush them with oil.

10. Bake the egg rolls for 10 minutes or until they are golden brown. If you'd like, serve them with cilantro and fresh vegetables on the side!

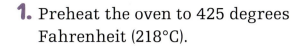

Read More

America's Test Kitchen. *The Complete DIY Cookbook for Young Chefs*. Boston: America's Test Kitchen, 2020.

Gifford, Clive, and Jacqueline Meldrum. *Living on the Veg: A Kids' Guide to Life without Meat*. Minneapolis: Free Spirit Publishing, 2019.

Sohn, Emily, and Diane Bair. *Food and Nutrition*. Chicago: Norwood House Press, 2020.

Internet Sites

Being a Vegetarian
kidshealth.org/en/teens/vegetarian.html

Vegetarian Kids' Recipes
bbcgoodfood.com/recipes/collection/vegetarian-kids-recipes

What Is a Vegan?
wonderopolis.org/wonder/What-Is-a-Vegan

About the Author

Tami grew up eating only peanut butter and jelly sandwiches and mac and cheese. It wasn't until she was an adult that food sparked her interest. Since then, she has thrown herself into trying new foods and improving every recipe she can find. She lives in Minnesota with her husband, two daughters, and a big orange cat.